WORKING ANIMALS

Helpers

WORKING ANIMALS

Helpers

Claudia Martin

Marshall Cavendish
Benchmark
New York

This edition first published by Marshall Cavendish Benchmark in 2011
Copyright © 2011 Amber Books Ltd

Published by Marshall Cavendish Benchmark
An imprint of Marshall Cavendish Corporation

Website: www.marshallcavendish.us

This publication represents the opinions and views of the author based on Claudia Martin's personal experience, knowledge, and research. The information in this book serves as a general guide only. The author and publisher have used their best efforts in preparing this book and disclaim liability rising directly and indirectly from the use and application of this book.

Other Marshall Cavendish Offices:
Marshall Cavendish International (Asia) Private Limited, 1 New Industrial Road, Singapore 536196 • Marshall Cavendish International (Thailand) Co Ltd. 253 Asoke, 12th Flr, Sukhumvit 21 Road, Klongtoey Nua, Wattana, Bangkok 10110, Thailand • Marshall Cavendish (Malaysia) Sdn Bhd, Times Subang, Lot 46, Subang Hi-Tech Industrial Park, Batu Tiga, 40000 Shah Alam, Selangor Darul Ehsan, Malaysia

Marshall Cavendish is a trademark of Times Publishing Limited

All websites were available and accurate when this book was sent to press.

Library of Congress Cataloging-in-Publication Data

Martin, Claudia.
  Helpers / Claudia Martin.
      p. cm. – (Working animals)
  Includes index.
  Summary: "Describes animals that help people who are blind or deaf, or who have physical handicaps"–Provided by publisher.
  ISBN 978-1-60870-163-6
  1. Animals as aids for people with disabilities–Juvenile literature. 2. Animals–Therapeutic use–Juvenile literature. 3. Working animals–Juvenile literature. 4. Service dogs–Juvenile literature. I. Title.
  HV1569.6.M35 2010
  362.4'078–dc22
                            2010006404

Editorial and design by
Amber Books Ltd
Bradley's Close
74–77 White Lion Street
London N1 9PF
United Kingdom
www.amberbooks.co.uk

Project Editor: James Bennett
Copy Editor: Peter Mavrikis
Design: Andrew Easton
Picture Research: Terry Forshaw, Natascha Spargo

Printed in China
135642

CONTENTS

Chapter 1
Helping the Blind

Imagine what it would feel like to walk down a crowded street without being able to see. Now imagine that your only companion was not a person, but a dog! Guide dogs help people who are blind to get about and perform everyday tasks.

Many blind people are able to hold demanding jobs and lead active lives, thanks to their guide dogs. They are able, for example, to get safely to and from work, or to and from school to pick up their children. Not everyone who uses a guide dog is completely blind. Some people, considered visually impaired, have limited vision and can see light and dark areas or objects when they are very close up.

A guide dog is trained to know the routes that its owner, or handler, walks

◄ **Labrador retrievers are the most popular breed of guide dog.**

▲ **A guide dog wears a special harness when it is working.**

regularly. Once outside, the dog is equipped with a **harness** that the handler holds on to. The dog cannot make decisions like a human being. Rather, the handler makes the choices and gives the dog simple commands. The handler acts like someone reading a map in the passenger seat of a car, giving directions to the driver. The dog is like the driver. It must follow the directions and make sure the journey is a safe one.

Three Important Tasks

A guide dog is trained to accomplish three important tasks. The first is to

▼ A guide dog helps its owner get about. Here they ride an escalator.

A Special Bond

The relationship between a guide dog and owner is very special. Each time the pair leaves the house, the owner puts total trust in the dog. Sometimes a blind person may feel isolated, or cut off, from the world. It can be very hard to meet new people or find a job when you cannot see. A guide dog can offer friendship and companionship. Having such a trusted friend can give a blind person confidence when approaching a new situation, such as attending the first day of school or starting a new job. In fact, guide dog organizations report that blind people who use guide dogs are more likely to have a job than blind people who do not.

For this special relationship to work, a dog needs to feel happy and valued, too. Usually only blind people over the age of sixteen or eighteen can be trained to work with a guide dog. This is because the training takes a level of discipline and responsibility that often only comes with age.

▲ **Guide dogs and owners form close, lasting relationships.**

▲ **A guide dog concentrates on helping its owner board a train to work.**

▶ **A guide dog stops at a curb to allow its owner to listen for traffic.**

help its owner avoid obstacles in the street. These obstacles might be stationary, such as a lamppost, a pothole, or an overhanging tree branch. Or they might be moving, such as pedestrians, wheelchairs, or strollers. A guide dog steers its owner safely around all of these hazards.

To accomplish this task, the dog has to have mastered a skill called "intelligent disobedience." This means it needs to learn when to refuse its owner's command—when

Did You Know

Guide Dog Qualities

Not all dogs are suited to being guide dogs. A guide dog trainer will look for these qualities:

- A gentle temperament.
- Calmness when introduced to loud noises, crowds, and other animals.
- Intelligence, a good memory, and an ability to learn complex skills.
- Excellent concentration.

What Causes Blindness?

Some people are born with a condition that causes blindness, while other people lose their sight due to disease or injury. In the developing world, the most common causes of blindness are disease and malnutrition (poor diet or lack of food). With proper medical care and diet, most cases of blindness in the developing world could be avoided.

Around half the blind people in the world have a condition called cataracts. This is when the lens of the eye clouds over, eventually causing loss of sight. Cataracts can be removed by an operation, but many people in poorer nations do not get this chance.

In places such as the United States and Europe, one of the most common causes of blindness is glaucoma. Glaucoma is a group of diseases that affect the optic nerve—the nerve that carries messages from the eye to the brain. Some people also experience vision loss as they enter old age. Blindness is rare, but we should all think about protecting our eyes by making sure that we eat healthy foods and take basic safety precautions. It is important to wear sunglasses to protect your eyes from strong sunlight in the summer. We should also always wear goggles when we're making home improvements. And don't delay that eye test! Spotting a problem early can prevent it from getting worse.

▲ **Paula Abdul donates a guide dog to visually impaired *American Idol* contestant Scott MacIntyre, on behalf of Guide Dogs of America.**

"With proper medical care and diet, most cases of blindness in the developing world could be avoided."

there is danger present, for example, such as an oncoming car at a street crossing.

The second key task for a guide dog is to make its owner aware of any change in elevation, or ground level. It might, for example, indicate that the owner has reached a flight of stairs or the edge of a train platform. The dog signals these changes by stopping or sitting down. If the pair comes to a curb, the dog will alert the owner to listen for traffic or the automated crossing signal.

▼ **The most common breeds selected to be guide dogs are German shepherds, golden retrievers, and Labrador retrievers.**

The third important task for a guide dog is to locate objects and places upon command. Inside the house, the dog might simply pick up a dropped newspaper or bring in the mail from the front door. Outside the home, the dog might take its owner to the entrance or exit of a room or building. Or it might indicate where the owner can find a doorknob or the button to summon an elevator. When commanded, a guide dog can follow a waiter to a restaurant table or a shop assistant to a particular shelf. With a well-trained guide dog, a blind person can find his or her way in all sorts of unfamiliar places.

Training Guide Dogs

Dogs are usually trained by special guide dog organizations. Most of these organizations are charities, which rely on donations to carry out their work. They help many people

◄ **Dogs begin their training early, while they are still puppies. But not all of them make it to become guide dogs.**

▲ **A trainer instructs her canine pupil while holding it firmly by the harness.**

« At training school, the dog learns all the skills it will need to work as a guide dog. »

who could not otherwise afford the expense of a guide dog.

Guide dog organizations usually breed their own dogs. A puppy stays with its mother until it is six weeks old. It then goes to live with a puppy walker, who introduces the young dog to the outside world. The walker

If You See a Guide Dog

If you happen to see an owner and guide dog when you are out, remember that the dog's concentration is vital. Do not distract the dog by petting it. A guide dog owner may sometimes require additional assistance when crossing a busy street or boarding a train. If you think help is needed, do not be embarrassed to ask. If your offer is accepted, let the owner take your arm.

takes the puppy along busy streets and leads it onto buses and trains. The puppy now has a chance to get used to human company. It is taught simple commands such as "sit," "stay," and "come." When the puppy reaches one year of age, the walker has to say goodbye, and the dog goes on to training school.

At training school, the dog learns all the skills it will need to work as a guide dog. Training can take up to six months. The training to become a guide dog is challenging, and not all the young dogs will see it through to the final goal.

Some dogs will reveal that they are not suited to the demanding role of a guide dog. Some of these dogs will be retrained as service dogs for deaf people or as medical assistance dogs. Others will become

▶ **A trainer puts a dog through its paces on an obstacle course.**

"Retired guide dogs are often in great demand as pets, and they are always relocated to loving homes."

companions for children who are blind or visually impaired.

A Working Dog

After completing the training, a successful dog meets its owner. Dogs and owners are matched carefully, depending on the owner's height, length of walking stride, and lifestyle. Now the new team of handler and dog receives about four weeks of training together. When the team has mastered all its skills, the new guide dog gets to go home with its owner. The team will be visited regularly by trainers to help with any new situations that the owner might face, such as moving to a new neighborhood or changing jobs.

The work of a guide dog is very demanding. Most guide dogs retire after about seven years of service. An owner often keeps the retired dog as a pet, while training a younger dog in harness. But since an owner may work with as many as six or seven dogs over the course of a lifetime, it is not always possible for the retired dog to stay on. This makes for a very sad time for both owner and dog. Retired guide dogs, however, are often in great demand as pets, and they are always relocated to loving homes. Some may even return to the home of their original puppy walker.

A Breed Apart

Some breeds of dog are more likely to make good guide dogs than others. Dog breeds have been developed by humans over hundreds of years to create animals that have particular skills and temperaments. The breeds most commonly chosen to be guide

◄ Guide dog charities usually breed their own puppies, such as this golden retriever. One family can provide generations of guide dogs.

"Yorkshire terriers, collies, and even Doberman pinschers have all been successfully trained to be guides."

Did You Know?

• There are about 1.3 million blind people in the United States and only about 7,000 guide dog users. Guide dog charities are always in need of support to help more blind people get the assistance they need.

• Not all blind people use a guide dog to help them get around. Many people use a cane. This is swung in front of the walker to feel for any obstacles.

• All over the world there are blind people who never go out alone. This is particularly the case in developing countries, where people do not have access to trained dogs or other assistance.

dogs are golden retrievers, Labrador retrievers, and German shepherds, because of their gentleness and intelligence. Labradoodles are also a popular choice. These dogs are part Labrador retriever and part poodle. Like poodles, the dogs don't shed much hair, making them better suited to people with allergies. Although less commonly selected, Yorkshire terriers, collies, and even Doberman pinschers have all been successfully trained to be guides.

Guide Horses?

Because they are intelligent and loyal, dogs have long made the best guide animals. Recently, however, miniature horses have been tried out as guide animals. Miniature horses, the result of several hundred years of **selective breeding**, are tiny: less than 26

▶ **Miniature horses are also trained to work as guide animals. Horses such as Tonto receive a year of training before meeting their owners.**

inches (66 centimeters) tall. They have the advantage of being helpful to blind people who are allergic to dogs or afraid of them. They also have longer working lives than dogs. A miniature horse can work for thirty years, as opposed to a guide dog's seven. But miniature horses can only be used by people who have plenty of space for a stable and land to roam. Some people are opposed to the use of miniature horses because they believe that they are not as reliable as dogs and can cause accidents.

History of Guide Dogs

No one knows exactly when dogs were first used to assist the blind. There is a picture of a blind person being led by a dog on the wall of a building in the ancient Roman town of Herculaneum. It was painted nearly two thousand years ago. The first known organized attempt to train guide dogs occurred in Paris in the 1780s.

The story of modern guide dogs starts during World War I (1914–1918). Thousands of German soldiers lost their sight in battle. A doctor named Gerhard Stalling had an idea to train dogs to help these men. He set up a series of guide dog schools across Germany. An American, Dorothy Eustis, was so impressed by Stalling's work that she wrote an article about the schools in a U.S. newspaper. At the time, Eustis was living in Switzerland, where she trained dogs for the police and army. A blind American named Morris Frank soon learned about her article and suggested that they work together to introduce guide dogs to the United States. As a result of their collaboration, America's first guide dog, Buddy, traveled across the Atlantic. Guide dog schools soon opened throughout the United States and around the world, forever changing the lives of blind people.

▶ **America's first guide dog was a German shepherd named Buddy. In 1928 Buddy started to work with owner Morris Frank.**

Chapter 2
Working with the Deaf

Dogs that are trained to alert deaf people to common sounds are known as hearing dogs. These working animals provide a great service to people with hearing problems, helping them become more independent and keeping them safe.

Most hearing dogs are trained to respond to six common sounds in the home: fire and smoke alarms, telephone rings, oven timers, alarm clocks, doorbells or door knocks, and having their name called. A dog that is placed with a deaf person who has a baby can also be trained to respond to the baby's cry. To make the owner aware of a sound, the dog will either jump on the owner, nudging with its nose, or simply paw the person. The dog will then lead the deaf person to the

◀ **Hearing dogs live with their owners and help make their homes safe.**

▲ **When the alarm clock goes off, this hearing dog will alert its owner. Time to get up!**

Life Saver!

There are stories from around the world about hearing dogs that have saved their owners' lives. One dog, a Cavalier King Charles spaniel named Lye, has become a hero several times over.

In one of her first acts of bravery, Lye saved her owner, forty-year-old Nicola, from intruders who were breaking into her house. Another time, Lye's barking brought quick help after Nicola collapsed in an alley. And one night, Lye even saved Nicola's daughter's life.

Fifteen-year-old Josie-Ann had begun to choke on a drink while her mother and Lye were asleep upstairs. Lye was awakened by the noise and rushed downstairs to see what was going on. Josie-Ann was able to signal to Lye that she needed help. The brave dog rushed straight back upstairs and woke Nicola, who phoned for an ambulance and gave her daughter life-saving first aid.

source of the sound. In the case of a fire alarm, of course, a dog is trained to lead its owner away from danger.

Once placed with its owner, a dog can be trained to respond to other sounds, such as a whistling tea kettle or a beeping microwave oven. In fact, a hearing dog, as long as it is well taught, can alert its owner to any sound.

Outside the Home

Some highly skilled hearing dogs can work outside the home. While they are not taught to alert their owners to specific sounds as they are in the home, these hearing dogs are trained to look at possible hazards. For example, when a hearing dog turns to look at a honking car, the owner can also turn to see a possible source of danger. This helps make owners much more aware of their surroundings.

When hearing dogs are out and about, they can often be identified by

▶ **Hearing dogs can be identified by an orange collar and vest. They have been helping deaf people for more than thirty years.**

> *"A hearing dog, as long as it is well taught, can alert its owner to any sound."*

an orange collar and leash or a special vest. Hearing dogs, along with other service animals, are allowed by law to enter any store that serves the public, including restaurants, clothing stores, and sporting arenas, where ordinary pets are not admitted.

A Hearing Dog's Training

Organizations that train hearing dogs often rescue their animals from

▼ **A hearing dog can belong to any breed, but it should be gentle, intelligent, and dedicated to its work.**

▶ **Hearing dogs can go where ordinary pets cannot. Ready to board a plane with its owner, this dog sits patiently as it is weighed in.**

"From the start, every hearing dog is trained in basic obedience. "

shelters. Shelters care for homeless or abused animals. The dogs chosen to be hearing dogs are picked for their friendliness, confidence, and physical condition. They come from a variety of breeds, but are usually small to medium-sized so that they will be comfortable in an average home.

From the start, every hearing dog is trained in basic obedience. It is also

▼ It can cost as much as $10,000 to train a hearing dog, but most charities supply dogs to their owners free of charge.

socialized, which means it is encouraged to get used to all the things it will encounter in the future, such as traffic, other animals, and different people. After this, each dog begins its basic sound training, which takes from four to six months to complete.

Pairing Up

After finishing basic sound training, a dog will meet its human partner for

▲ **Sometimes specially trained hearing dogs are placed with deaf children. These dogs may be called "team hearing dogs," because they work with both the child and the parents.**

"Even if there are other people living in the home, the owner takes full responsibility for the dog's exercise and care."

the first time. Each dog's skills and personality will have been matched with a deaf person's lifestyle, personality, and home. Hearing dogs are usually placed with people who are over sixteen, as it takes a lot of self-discipline to work with a hearing dog. After working with the dog at the training school, the owner can take it home. But the training isn't done yet. Owner and animal helper face an additional year of lessons to get them fully compatible. During this time, a dog trainer will make regular visits to help the team develop its skills.

Owner and animal helper usually form a loving friendship. Even if there are other people living in the home, the owner takes full responsibility for the dog's exercise and care. That helps to make sure the dog is dedicated to its owner alone.

From Hollywood to Hearing Dogs

What links Hollywood with the very first dogs for the deaf? The answer is an animal trainer named Roy Kabat. Together with an audiologist (someone who helps people with hearing difficulties) and the animal welfare group American Humane Society, Kabat began training hearing dogs in the mid-1970s. Kabat had previously trained animals for circuses as well as famous Hollywood films such as *Dr. Doolittle* (1967), about a veterinarian who can talk with animals, and *Born Free* (1966), about an orphaned lion cub. Now his team came up with a successful dog-training program and established the charity Dogs for the Deaf in 1977. Kabat chose his dogs from local animal shelters, saying, "They're the dogs that otherwise might be put to sleep." The system set up by Kabat was copied around the world.

Learning to Work Together

- During training, the owner practices common sounds daily so that the dog can get used to them.
- Whenever the dog alerts the owner to a sound, the owner must immediately follow the dog to the sound (unless it's a fire alarm).
- The dog is rewarded after it performs each exercise well.

▲ **During training, an owner asks, "What is it?" after the dog has pawed her to indicate that it has heard a sound. Then the dog shows her what it is: a ringing telephone.**

Chapter 3
More Service Animals

Animals can help people in many different ways, some of them pretty amazing. There are animals that help their owners to move about, or be mobile. Other service animals help people who suffer from diseases or mental health problems.

Mobility Assistance Dogs

Mobility assistance dogs help people who have **disabilities** that make it hard for them to move around or manage physical tasks. The skills that a dog is trained to perform depend on its owner's needs. Around the house, a dog might help retrieve objects such as car keys, television remotes, and books. Some mobility assistance dogs can turn lights on and off or open and close doors and drawers. Some can even load and unload a washing machine, or put garbage into the trash bin. Dogs can help their owners undress by gently pulling off shoes, socks, and jackets.

◄ **Mobility assistance dogs often work with wheelchair users.**

▲ **A golden retriever picks up its owner's dropped book.**

Monkey Helpers

Monkey helpers are specially trained monkeys that work with people who have severe disabilities such as quadriplegia (the loss of the use of both arms and legs). Usually, Capuchin monkeys, known for their intelligence and **dexterity**, are chosen. The monkeys live in a human home from a very early age, so that they are thoroughly used to people. After about seven years of training in a special school, a monkey helper can aid its owner with tasks such as opening jars, microwaving food, and brushing hair.

▼ **This capuchin monkey has been trained to use a cloth to rub its owner's face.**

❝Dogs can help their owners undress by gently pulling off shoes, socks, and jackets.❞

▲ **Leon helps his owner, Katrina, take off her shoes. Leon has lived with Katrina since he was two years old.**

On shopping trips, a mobility assistance dog can be trained to hand over money at the counter. It can even remove products from a store shelf and put them into a shopping cart. If they're light, the purchases can be carried home by the dog in a pack.

Mobility assistance dogs often work with people who use wheelchairs.

"On shopping trips, a mobility assistance dog can be trained to hand over money at the counter."

These dogs can help their owners get in and out of the chair. Some larger dogs can be fitted with a special harness to tow the wheelchair. Specially trained "walker" dogs help people who have difficulty walking. The owners can gently lean on them to keep their balance.

In addition to all their many skills, mobility assistance dogs are trained to respond to accidents and other dangerous situations—they bark loudly for help!

The puppies that are selected for this work are usually adopted from animal shelters. They must be gentle

A Parrot Helper

One of the most unusual animal helpers is a parrot. Her name is Sadie. She is the constant companion of Jim Eggers, a man who suffers from bipolar disorder. This malady causes a person to suffer extreme mood swings, from deep depressions to "manic" highs. During Jim's manic periods, he would feel angry and behave wildly, which sometimes led to his getting into trouble with the police. Then, during one of these periods, he noticed that his talking pet parrot began to repeat phrases to him over and over, making him feel calmer. Sadie might say things like "Calm down, it's okay" or "I love you." These were words that Jim had expressed to her when he was feeling well. Jim found that Sadie's "parroting" helped him a lot. Now Sadie goes everywhere with him, making her the only known service parrot on record.

▶ **A mobility assistance dog helps its owner with the grocery shopping, selecting food both for the owner and himself!**

" Some service dogs are trained to help people with medical problems. They are especially good in emergencies. "

and intelligent but also strong. Breeds such as Labradors and golden retrievers are often chosen. Dogs are usually trained for about one year before they are matched with an owner. Not all mobility assistance dogs are trained by an organization, however. Some owners are able to do the training themselves.

Medical Response Dogs

Some service dogs are trained to help people with medical problems. They

▲ A medical response dog always has to be alert to its owner's state of health—but dog and owner can still find time to play.

▶ Toby was rescued from an animal shelter. He is being trained to raise the alarm if his owner, who suffers from diabetes, loses consciousness.

« Medical response dogs warn the owners so that they can eat something to give them more glucose. »

are especially good in emergencies. Some know how to alert their owner to a dangerous change in his or her medical condition. Some are trained to bring their owner a telephone in case of an emergency.

Medical response dogs are often partnered with people who have diabetes. Diabetes is a condition in which the body is slow in using glucose, a type of sugar that is our chief source of energy. If glucose builds up in the blood, a person can become dangerously ill. People with diabetes are treated for this problem and their glucoses levels are monitored carefully. Sometimes, however, a diabetic's glucose levels can actually fall too low. That's when a medical response dog can be of invaluable help. Dogs trained to work with diabetics are taught to

▲ **This golden retriever is trained to help elderly people with Alzheimer's disease, which can cause confusion, memory loss, and stress.**

Dogs for Veterans

Today thousands of American military personnel are facing danger in Afghanistan and Iraq. Some of these soldiers are returning home with serious injuries, such as blindness, loss of limbs, and paralysis. Guide dogs and mobile assistance dogs are needed more than ever. This extra need is being met not only by the government but by various organizations, such as Veterans Helping Today's Returning Heroes. Assisted by their animal helpers, injured veterans are getting a chance to make a new start in life.

▲ **Ryan served in the armed forces in Iraq, where he was injured. Today he trains service dogs to help other veterans.**

Trained in Prison

In the United States and Australia, some service dogs are trained by prison inmates. They teach the dogs obedience skills and help them master the special tasks they will be required to do in their future work. An inmate training a dog meant for someone with epilepsy, for example, will teach it how to bark when its owner has a seizure.

The inmates who volunteer for these training programs enjoy being with animals. The job can give them a sense of purpose and can be very satisfying. They know that the animals they train will be helping people with disabilities lead more independent and productive lives.

▲ Hundreds of service dogs are trained by prison inmates every year, including this Labrador, who is learning to be a mobility assistance dog.

notice the very faint smell that their owners' bodies give off when their glucose levels have fallen. The dogs warn the owners so that they can eat something to give them more glucose.

Some medical response dogs are trained to help people who have epilepsy. Epileptics suffer from seizures. During a seizure, a person loses consciousness and has **convulsions**. Dogs are taught to summon help when this happens. They will also pull any dangerous objects away from the owner, since the person is not in control of his movements. Some dogs are so sensitive to their owners that they develop the ability to alert them before they have a seizure.

Psychiatric Assistance Dogs

Psychiatric assistance dogs are trained to help owners with such mental health problems as severe depression or schizophrenia [skit-so-FREE-nee-uh]. Schizophrenia is a disorder that may cause the sufferer to experience **hallucinations** and to have confused speech and thinking. Dogs can be taught to remind their

owners to take their medications. They may also guide them away from stressful situations, and try to prevent them from carrying out repetitive behavior caused by their illness.

▼ **Milo is the constant companion of Hannah, who has epilepsy. He is trained to alert her to a possible seizure wherever they may be.**

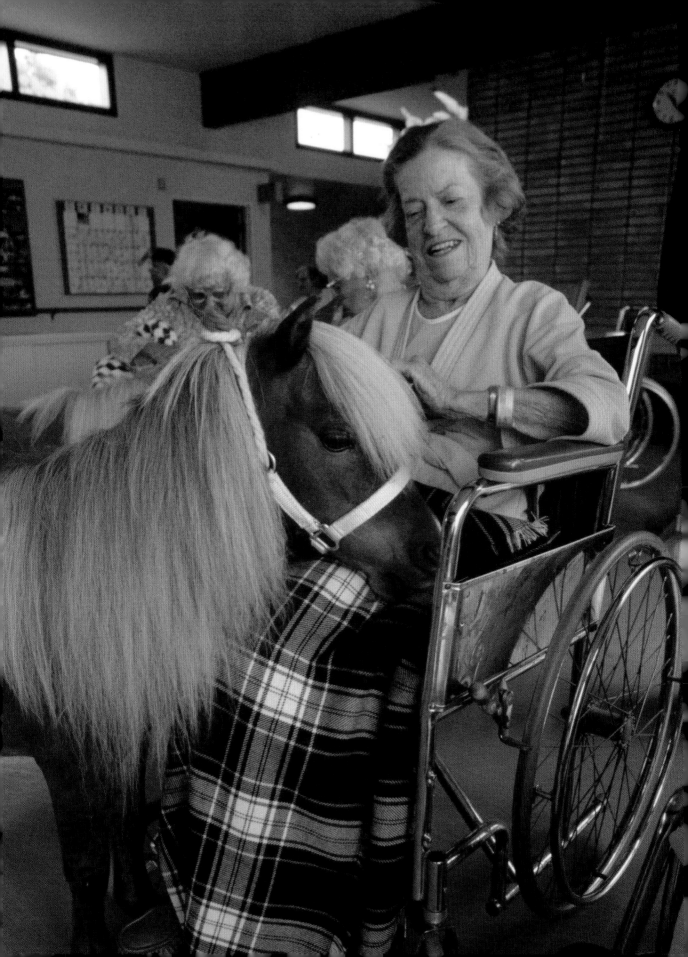

Chapter 4
Animal Therapy

Most people find that stroking an animal makes them feel happier. Doctors have noticed that people who are ill feel less anxious and grow more confident when they spend time with an animal on a regular basis.

When people feel happier and better about themselves, they often start to feel better physically. These discoveries have led to the use of animal-assisted therapy around the world.

All the animals that work in animal-assisted therapy are gentle and friendly. Many different kinds of animals are used for therapy— from dogs, cats, rabbits, and guinea pigs to horses, birds, and even reptiles.

Therapy animals are often taken to places where people might benefit from their comforting presence. These can include schools for children with special needs or the children's wards of hospitals. Elderly

◄ **A miniature horse is a popular visitor at retirement homes.**

▲ **Regular time with an animal can benefit children with special needs.**

> **Therapy animals are often taken to places where people might benefit from their comforting presence.**

people also enjoy animal company, so therapy animals are taken to retirement homes, nursing homes, and hospices.

A disaster area is one of the most demanding places for a therapy animal. After experiencing an earthquake, flood, or other natural disaster, people are in shock and

▶ **Petting a gentle animal like a guinea pig can be relaxing and comforting.**

Smoky the Yorkie

One of the first famous therapy animals was a Yorkshire terrier named Smoky. His owner, Corporal William Wynne, was wounded while fighting in the Philippines during World War II (1939–1945). While Wynne was recovering in an army hospital, his friends brought in Smoky to cheer him up. Smoky was a big hit with all the other wounded soldiers on the ward, so the doctor in charge decided to take the pet on his rounds. Smoky continued his work as a therapy dog after the war was over.

▶ **In Cleveland, Ohio, a life-size statue commemorates Smoky, along with other working dogs that have served in wartime.**

SMOKY

YORKIE DOODLE DANDY
AND
DOGS OF ALL WARS

need help to recover. When Hurricane Katrina hit New Orleans in 2005, many survivors were left feeling lost and frightened. Petting therapy dogs helped ease their anxieties. The trained therapists who worked with the dogs also reported that people seemed more willing to talk about their feelings in the presence of a friendly pet.

Many animals working in animal-assisted therapy are the personal pets of their handlers. They may just make weekly visits to the places where they are needed. Others are dedicated to their work full-time.

▲ **Therapy dogs provide warmth and comfort to people suffering from the shock of a natural disaster. Children as well as adults can easily become attached to these pets.**

Riding for the Disabled

Many therapy programs give disabled adults and children the opportunity to ride horses. This is called equine-assisted therapy. Physically disabled people can work on their mobility and coordination skills by riding and grooming the horses. The most skilled riders often enter competitions with other disabled riders, sometimes at an international level. If a person is not physically able to ride a horse, he or she may go carriage driving, which takes plenty of coordination and balance. When people have to use a lot of machinery and equipment in their daily lives, such as wheelchairs or crutches, they really enjoy the chance to have contact with a warm, living animal.

Mentally disabled people can benefit from equine-assisted therapy, too. When they participate in a program, they get a chance to meet new people and acquire new skills, such as caring for a horse or pony. They also get the chance to have fun out in the fresh air.

▲ **Equine-assisted therapy works well for most disabled people. Youngsters love riding and grooming the horses.**

Comforting Companions

Some therapy animals live with the people they help. People with mental illness, such as those suffering from depression, benefit from living with specially trained pets. Animals that work in this field are sometimes called "career change" service animals; they were, at first, trained to help blind, deaf, or disabled people but were not entirely suitable.

Children with autism can benefit greatly from having a pet. Autism is a disorder that affects a person's ability to communicate and interact with others. A six-year-old autistic boy named William, for example, was given a Labrador retriever named Percy. Percy was specially trained to work with autistic children. Within weeks of living with Percy, William showed more interest in talking with his teachers and his family members.

Swimming with Dolphins

Sometimes, children and adults with special needs are encouraged to swim with dolphins. It is believed that swimming alongside these intelligent and gentle animals can help with mental challenges such as depression or learning difficulties. Sometimes dolphin programs use captive dolphins that live in a large aquarium. Other times, people swim beside wild dolphins in the sea. However, many animal welfare groups feel that dolphins should be left in the wild and have as little human contact as possible. They fear that swimming beside wild dolphins can cause them to change their habits. In order to avoid humans, they may move away from areas where they usually rest or find food. This could endanger their survival. Some animal welfare campaigners even believe that swimming with a captive or wild dolphin could cause it stress or injury.

▶ **Frank suffers from depression, but he is already feeling happier after just two months of living with his friendly cocker spaniel, Topper.**

Chapter 5
Career Guide

If you love animals and enjoy helping people, a career working with service animals might be for you. You might enjoy training the animals. Or you might become a therapist, working with the animals and the people who need their help.

Puppy Walker

Becoming a puppy walker is a good way to gain experience in working with service animals. A puppy walker's role is important, because it helps dogs to become socialized, or comfortable with people and places—from shopping malls to train stations.

Puppy walkers are usually unpaid—they volunteer their time and energy—although they are given money to cover the cost of their puppy's food. Being a puppy walker

◀ **A therapist helps patient and service dog get acquainted.**

▲ **A guide-dog trainer teaches his pupil how to walk around obstacles.**

❝The hardest part is saying goodbye to the dog when it is a year old and ready to go on to further training.❞

takes huge commitment. The hardest part is saying goodbye to the dog when it is a year old and ready to go on to further training. If you think that you and your family can commit to puppy walking, contact your nearest service dog organization.

Animal Trainer

Guide dogs, hearing dogs, and other service animals are trained in special schools by qualified instructors. Trainers teach the animals all the skills they will need in their working life. They also match each animal with an

Do You Have What It Takes?

You could be just the right person to work with service animals. Do you think you have these qualities?

- A love of animals.
- A desire to work with people to help them get the most from their lives.
- Good communication skills, with both people and animals.
- Lots of patience—training an animal in special skills means you will always need to be calm, kind, and gentle.

▲ **Equine-therapy can be a rewarding career.**

owner, bearing in mind the owner's needs and lifestyle. Instructors then give training to the human-animal team. Most trainers have a high school diploma and many also complete specialized programs at service animal organizations.

Therapist

The easiest way to get involved in animal-assisted therapy is to offer your time as a volunteer. If you have a friendly and gentle pet, you can contact a pet therapy organization. (Don't forget to get your parents' permission first.) You and your pet will need to be carefully checked by the organization to make sure that you both will do your best to help the people you will serve. You may also have to take part in a training program. The organization will then

▲ A therapist may work within a hospital, planning programs and visiting with patients.

match you up with a local hospital, school, or nursing home that welcomes pet visits.

If you pursue a full-time career in animal-assisted therapy, you will get the chance to work with people with special needs or mental-health challenges. You will plan and direct activities with animals for patients in hospitals and other institutions. If you would like to work as a therapist, you must first complete high school and then study and become **licensed** in one of several fields, such as nursing, **social work**, or **psychological counseling**. You will then need extra training in order to use animals as part of your work.

▶ **Working with service animals and the people who need their help can be a satisfying career.**

Working for a Service Dog Organization

Service dog organizations offer a lot of different job opportunities. You might be:

• A veterinarian—a doctor who monitors the health of the dogs and treats them when they are sick.

• An animal care-giver—a person who feeds, exercises, and grooms the dogs, plus takes care of them when they are sick.

• An animal trainer—a person who teaches the dogs and matches them up with patients.

• A rehabilitation worker—a person who helps disabled people to develop their existing skills.

• A fundraiser—a person who sets up programs to get people to donate money to the organization and keep it in business.

• A press officer—a person who maintains contact with the media—newspapers, radio, television, the Internet—to keep the public aware of the good work of the organization.

Glossary

convulsions
violent, involuntary contractions of the muscles; spasms

dexterity
skill in using the hands

disabilities
physical or mental conditions that limit a person's activities

hallucinations
things seen or heard that are not real; delusions

harness
a special set of straps and wires fitted to a guide dog which allow the owner to sense its movements

licensed
having a certificate that shows you have legal permission to work at a particular job

psychiatric
having to do with treating emotional and mental disorders

psychological counseling
advice on mental and emotional problems

selective breeding
developing animals that have particular looks and characteristics through the mating of chosen individuals

social work
a career field that helps to improve the lives of people who are physically, mentally, or economically disadvantaged

Further Information

BOOKS

Kent, Deborah. *Animal Helpers for the Disabled*. New York: Franklin Watts, 2003.

McDaniel, Melissa and Wilma Melville. *Guide Dogs (Dog Heroes)*. New York: Bearport Publishing, 2005.

Murray, Julie. *Therapy Animals (Going to Work: Animal Edition)*. Edina, MA: Buddy Books, 2009.

Presnall, Judith. *Animals with Jobs: Capuchin Monkey Aides*. San Diego, CA: KidHaven Press, 2003.

Presnall, Judith. *Animals with Jobs: Hearing Dogs*. San Diego, CA: KidHaven Press, 2004.

Tagliaferro, Linda and Wilma Melville. *Service Dogs (Dog Heroes)*. New York: Bearport Publishing, 2005.

WEBSITES

www.afb.org

The American Foundation for the Blind website offers useful information on blindness and Braille as well as puzzles and games for children.

www.cci.org

The Canine Companions for Independence website provides information about how this organization trains service dogs and helps people with disabilities.

www.deltasociety.org

This organization offers stories and advice about animal-assisted therapy and information on how to get yourself and your pet registered to volunteer.

www.dogsforthedeaf.org

This organization provides information about training hearing dogs, as well as how volunteers can become involved.

www.guidedogsofamerica.org

A useful site for information about the training and breeding of guide dogs, with reading lists for teachers.

www.therapyanimals.org

If you would like to volunteer with your pet to become part of an animal-assisted therapy program, this website is a useful starting point. It has answers to many questions and provides links to other organizations.

Index

PICTURE CREDITS

The photographs in this book are used by permission and through the courtesy of:

ABOUT THE AUTHOR

Claudia Martin is an author and editor with many years of experience creating books for children about the natural world, society, and history. She has a keen interest in animals and their relationship with humans. Her most recent books about animals include *Picking Your Pet* and *The Big Book of Questions and Answers*.